25 Prayers to Christmas

PRAYING THROUGH
THE CHRISTMAS STORY

Chris Paavola

St. Mark Lutheran Church

BATTLE CREEK, MICHIGAN

St. Mark Lutheran Church
114 Minges Rd. E
Battle Creek, MI 49015

www.stmark.net

Ordering Information:

Quantity sales. Special discounts are available on quantity purchases by churches, associations, and others. For details, contact "Book Requests" at the address above.

25 Prayers to Christmas/Chris Paavola. 1st ed.

About this Book

I wrote *25 Prayers to Christmas* to help you prepare for Christmas by praying through the Christmas story. Each day progresses through Luke's gospel in a verse-by-verse style, followed by a written prayer prompted by the account.

I encourage you to read each day's prayers aloud. Not only will it help you stay focused, but you'll become familiar with incorporating the language of Scripture into your prayers. It's one thing to read Mary's or Simeon's prayer, it's another thing to use their words as your own!

The book is broken into five sections to help orient you to the story: prayers from Jerusalem (Luke 1:5-25), prayers from Nazareth (Luke 1:26-38), prayers from the hill country of Judea (Luke 1:39-79), prayers from Bethlehem (Luke 2:1-19), and then one final prayer from Jerusalem (Luke 2:22-32).

Whether for yourself, your small group, or your church, thank you for celebrating Christ's birth with *25 Prayers to Christmas.*

– Chris

Contents

JERUSALEM 6

December 1st A Prayer to Be Heard 8

December 2nd A Prayer to Bring Back Many 10

December 3rd A Prayer to Make Ready 11

December 4th A Prayer to Be Sent to Speak 12

December 5th A Prayer of Confession 13

December 6th A Prayer of Gratitude 14

NAZARETH 15

December 7th A Prayer for God's Presence 16

December 8th A Prayer for Wonder 17

December 9th A Prayer Against Fear 18

December 10th A Prayer for Jesus to Be Great 19

December 11th A Prayer for Power 20

December 12th A Prayer for Surrender 21

THE HILL COUNTRY OF JUDEA 22

December 13th A Prayer Against Hurry 23

December 14th A Prayer for the Holy Spirit 24

December 15th A Prayer for a Humble Heart...........25

December 16th A Prayer to Believe...........................26

December 17th Praying Mary's Song 27

December 18th A Prayer to Share the Joy 28

December 19th A Prayer of Praise 29

December 20th Praying Zechariah's Song.................31

BETHLEHEM 32

December 21st A Prayer for Generosity....................33

December 22nd A Prayer for Attention 35

December 23rd A Prayer for Peace.............................36

December 24th A Prayer to Treasure 37

A RETURN TO JERUSALEM 38

December 25th Praying Simeon's Song......................39

O Holy Child of Bethlehem,
descend to us, we pray.

- Phillips Brooks, O Little Town of Bethlehem, 1868

JERUSALEM

Luke 1:5-25

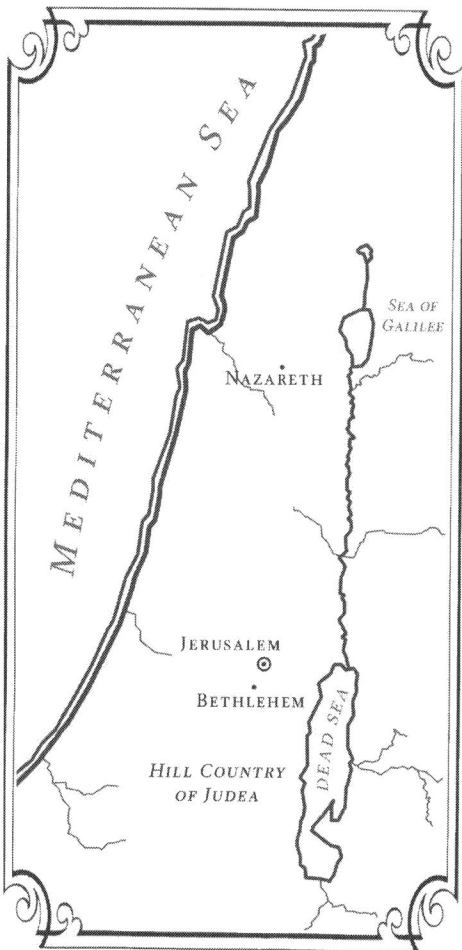

December 1st

A Prayer to Be Heard

Luke 1:5-13

⁵ In the time of Herod king of Judea there was a priest named Zechariah, who belonged to the priestly division of Abijah; his wife Elizabeth was also a descendant of Aaron. ⁶ Both of them were righteous in the sight of God, observing all the Lord's commands and decrees blamelessly. ⁷ But they were childless because Elizabeth was not able to conceive, and they were both very old.

⁸ Once when Zechariah's division was on duty and he was serving as priest before God, ⁹ he was chosen by lot, according to the custom of the priesthood, to go into the temple of the Lord and burn incense. ¹⁰ And when the time for the burning of incense came, all the assembled worshipers were praying outside.

¹¹ Then an angel of the Lord appeared to him, standing at the right side of the altar of incense. ¹² When Zechariah saw him, he was startled and was gripped with fear.

*¹³ But the angel said to him: "Do not be afraid, Zechariah; **your prayer has been heard**..."*

TODAY'S PRAYER:

Heavenly Father, you are the God who hears. Just as you heard the prayer of Zechariah and sent your messenger to appear to him, would you also hear the prayers I bring this season? Incline your ear to me, not because of any righteousness on my own, but because of your Son's righteousness alone.

I give you this day and this month to be a time of lifting my hands in prayer with all your people to call on your name.

Use the words and phrases from the account of your Son's birth to prompt my own prayers, deepen my faith, and enrich my Christmas celebration.

In Jesus' name. Amen.

December 2nd
A Prayer to Bring Back Many

Luke 1:13-16

[13] *"...Your wife Elizabeth will bear you a son, and you are to call him John.* [14] *He will be a joy and delight to you, and many will rejoice because of his birth,* [15] *for he will be great in the sight of the Lord. He is never to take wine or other fermented drink, and he will be filled with the Holy Spirit even before he is born.* [16] *He will* **bring back many** *of the people of Israel to the Lord their God."*

TODAY'S PRAYER:

Lord God, the Christmas season is a frantic season filled with decorations, music, and parties. Left unchecked, these activities overtake the meaning and message of your precious Son's birth.

This year, Lord, make it different. Make alive again the word the angel Gabriel spoke and bring the hearts of many to marvel and believe in the mystery of your Son's birth. In my home, in my church, in my community. Both those who have never believed and those who's faith has gone cold, let them come and behold him, born the King of Angels.

Enliven the dead heart, soften the callous heart, and give the gift of faith, Father. As we celebrate your Son's birth, may we also celebrate the second birth this Christmas of those who first believe. Bring back many to you, our Lord and God!

In Jesus' name. Amen.

December 3ʳᵈ

A Prayer to Make Ready

Luke 1:17
*¹⁷ "And he will go on before the Lord, in the spirit and power of Elijah, to turn the hearts of parents to their children and the disobedient to the wisdom of the righteous—to **make ready a people prepared for the Lord**."*

TODAY'S PRAYER:

God, I do many things to make ready my home to celebrate Christmas. But God, would you come with the spirit and power of Elijah, and the ministry of John the Baptist, and make ready my heart for your Son's arrival?

Where is my heart unprepared for the King's arrival?

Show me my sin, Lord. Show me where I have been greedy or vengeful. Take me further into my thoughts than I care to go and show me where I have been hateful, or even idolatrous. In the middle of the festivities of the season, make me penitent over my sin that requires a Savior to be sent at all.

And where I have been disobedient and unrighteous, cover me with the grace and mercy purchased for me by Christ Jesus. Make the crooked way straight. Make the rough way smooth. Prepare the way of the Lord that your Son may have the arrival his majesty deserves.

In Jesus' name. Amen.

December 4th

A Prayer to Be Sent to Speak

Luke 1:18-19 (CEB)
¹⁸ Zechariah said to the angel, "How can I be sure of this? My wife and I are very old."

*¹⁹ The angel replied, "I am Gabriel. I stand in God's presence. I was **sent to speak** to you and to bring this good news to you."*

TODAY'S PRAYER:

Lord, your angel Gabriel was a faithful messenger. First to Zechariah with the news of John's birth, and then to Mary with the news of Jesus' birth. Each time, he was faithful to both go and speak.

Lord, I know I am also sent to speak to the world you love with the good news of your Son's birth, but I often fail to do so. Forgive me for this and, as you forgive me, renew me to your task. Take away any fear or awkwardness I may have about speaking. Whether it's an invitation to worship with me, or an explanation of Jesus, give me the words to say. Help me to speak them calmly, gently, and clearly, as I ought. Help me be unafraid to say the name of Jesus.

In the same way, may those you send me to be receptive to your good news. Stir up a spiritual hunger and thirst in them. Give them the gift of faith, that they may call upon your name and be saved and share in the true joy of Christmas.

In Jesus' name. Amen.

December 5th

A Prayer of Confession

Luke 1:20-22
*²⁰ "And now you will be silent and not able to speak until the day this happens, **because you did not believe my words**, which will come true at their appointed time."*

²¹ Meanwhile, the people were waiting for Zechariah and wondering why he stayed so long in the temple. ²² When he came out, he could not speak to them. They realized he had seen a vision in the temple, for he kept making signs to them but remained unable to speak.

TODAY'S PRAYER:

God, not only have I failed to be as faithful as Zechariah with speaking your message, but I have also often failed to believe you and your Word.

I have doubted your goodness and done what was right in my own eyes. I have questioned your power and taken matters into my own hands. I have denied your timing and acted impatiently. I stand silent with Zechariah in the guilt of my disbelief.

[Take a moment to confess your doubt and disbelief to God.]

But just as your judgments are just, extend to me your mercy and grace. Forgive me and renew my faith, for the sake of your Son, whose birth I remember this season. Lord, I believe, help my unbelief!

In Jesus' name. Amen.

December 6th

A Prayer of Gratitude

Luke 1:23-25

*23 When his time of service was completed, he returned home. 24 After this his wife Elizabeth became pregnant and for five months remained in seclusion. 25 "**The Lord has done this for me**," she said. "In these days he has shown his favor and taken away my disgrace among the people."*

TODAY'S PRAYER:

Father, after Elizabeth's pregnancy in her old age, she gave thanks. She knew John's birth would not be possible without your provision.

This Christmas season, as I draw nearer to the matchless gift of your Son, I also give thanks to you for what you have given me. I have not earned or deserved the things I have, but I only have them because of your gracious and generous hand.

You have given me my loved ones, my shelter, my food, my job, my abilities, and my country. But even still, God, I thank you for...

[Take a moment to thank God for what he's given you.]

In Jesus' name. Amen.

NAZARETH

Luke 1:26-38

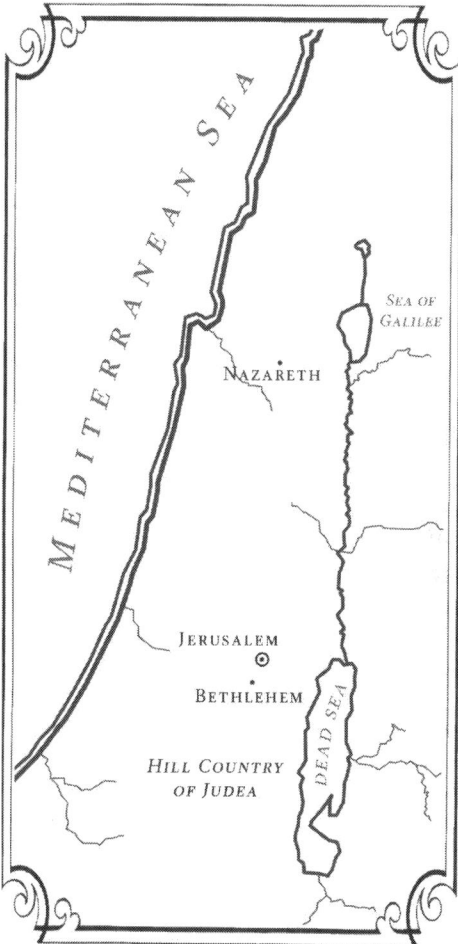

December 7th

A Prayer for God's Presence

Luke 1:26-28

*²⁶ In the sixth month of Elizabeth's pregnancy, God sent the angel Gabriel to Nazareth, a town in Galilee, ²⁷ to a virgin pledged to be married to a man named Joseph, a descendant of David. The virgin's name was Mary. ²⁸ The angel went to her and said, "Greetings, you who are highly favored! **The Lord is with you.**"*

TODAY'S PRAYER:

Most Holy God, you could have remained separate and distant from us in our sinful state. But in your great love, you looked on our helpless isolation and sent your Son, Immanuel, God With Us, to come to us that we might come to you. Oh, the bliss of this glorious thought!

In this moment, would you bring me a very real comfort with the knowledge of your very real presence? Remind my heart, my mind, my body—my entire soul, that I am not alone because you, the God of the universe, dwells with me.

In the same way, send your Comforter, your Spirit, to those who are suffering this season, especially...

[Take a moment to name those in need of God's comfort.]

Let us all know the same hope and joy Mary felt when she heard the good news that you are with us.

In Jesus' name. Amen.

December 8th

A Prayer for Wonder

Luke 1:29
[29] *Mary was **greatly troubled at his words and wondered** what kind of greeting this might be.*

TODAY'S PRAYER:

Lord, once Mary heard the angel's greeting, she knew she was being called and summoned to your purpose.

Yet while her mind flooded with questions, her wonder was never doubtful. Her wonder was expectant. Despite what she didn't know, she did know with certainty that you could do what you would declare, and no plan of yours could be thwarted. As your Son would later proclaim, "What is impossible with man is possible with God." (Luke 18:27)

Would you please give me this same faith in my wondering this Christmas? To wonder with faith at your Word made flesh. To wonder at how the virgin sings a lullaby. To wonder at how God is pleased as man with man to dwell.

And may my wondering at the miracles of Christmas lead me to a new year of faith, trusting in your faithfulness and power to accomplish all that you have promised for me. Instead of fear or doubt, to look forward to the future with faith-filled wondering.

In Jesus' name. Amen.

December 9th
A Prayer Against Fear

Luke 1:30
*³⁰ But the angel said to her, "**Do not be afraid**, Mary;
you have found favor with God.*

TODAY'S PRAYER:

Heavenly Father, beneath the frenzy of the Christmas season, there's a brooding sense of fear. We brighten the longer evenings with strings of lights, we color the gray of winter with vibrant decorations, because there is a lingering sense of things beyond our control. This is fear. Fear of loss, isolation, worthlessness, pain, or even death.

If I quiet myself long enough I can look beneath my worries and find the underlying fears I try to ignore or silence. Especially my fear of...

[Take a moment to confess your specific fears.]

But when your angel Gabriel appeared to Mary, he told her, "Do not be afraid." Lord, would you come by your Holy Spirit right now and speak those same words to me?

Tell me to fear not—because you are with me. Tell me to be strong and courageous—because you are greater than everything I fear. Every fear, from the small to the great, has been conquered by your Son, whose birth I celebrate this season. You are my light and my salvation—whom shall I fear?

In Jesus' name. Amen.

December 10th

A Prayer for Jesus to Be Great

Luke 1:31-33
*³¹ You will conceive and give birth to a son, and you are to call him Jesus. ³² **He will be great** and will be called the Son of the Most High. The Lord God will give him the throne of his father David, ³³ and he will reign over Jacob's descendants forever; his kingdom will never end."*

TODAY'S PRAYER:

Most High God, this Christmas season, make great the name of Jesus. Raise up him who descended for us.

I join John the Baptist and pray, even if I must decrease, he must increase! Make me last, that he who made himself last may be first. Make me least, that he who made himself least may be most. Make me small that he who made himself small may be great. Lift his name above all other names, especially my own.

This season celebrates Christ, who did not grasp equality with you and made himself nothing, taking on the nature of a servant. God, help me to follow my Lord's example. Teach me to set aside all self-promotion, self-importance, and self-interests. The student is not above the teacher, the servant is not above the master.

My calendar sets a celebration of Christ as Lord this season, help my life to do so as well. May he be highly exalted, make his name great!

In Jesus' name. Amen.

A Prayer for Power

Luke 1:34-37
³⁴ "How will this be," Mary asked, "since I am a virgin?"

*³⁵ The angel answered, "The Holy Spirit will come on you, and **the power of the Most High will overshadow you**. So the holy one to be born will be called the Son of God.*
³⁶ Even Elizabeth your relative is going to have a child in her old age, and she who was said to be unable to conceive is in her sixth month. ³⁷ For no word from God will ever fail."

TODAY'S PRAYER:

Heavenly Father, by your power, your Son was made man in a virgin's womb. By your same power, you raised him from the dead.

I want to know your power this Christmas season.

Give me the power to leave any habitual sin. Give me your power to forgive those who do not deserve it. Grant me, O Lord, the power to rejoice in difficult circumstances. Give me the power to stay faithful to your plans and your commands. Give me the power to wait patiently for you instead of taking matters into my own hands. Give me the power to grasp your love for me.

And when others ask me how it was done, may I answer that it was you and your power that made it possible, so you alone may have the glory, God.

In Jesus' name. Amen.

December 12th

A Prayer for Surrender

Luke 1:38 (GW)
[38] *Mary answered, "**I am the Lord's servant. Let everything you've said happen to me**." Then the angel left her.*

TODAY'S PRAYER:

Lord, I want to kneel with Mary this Christmas and proclaim that I am your servant, but I confess it's hard for me.

The thought of being a servant, bonded and captive to you, wages war with my pride and sensibilities. I would rather call you *Father,* or *God,* than to come under your sovereignty and control and submit to you as my *Lord* and *Master.* And yet these are the very titles your Son and his mother gave to you.

So, Lord, not my will, but thy will be done.

Whatever calling you've given me, thy will be done. Whatever difficult circumstances I find myself in— my relationships, my health, my finances—thy will be done. Change what is within your will to change, but what must remain, let it remain. I do not get to decide how your power, your grace, or your mercy are demonstrated in my life this Christmas season, only if they are.

I am your servant. Let everything you have said happen to me.

In Jesus' name. Amen.

THE HILL COUNTRY
OF JUDEA

Luke 1:39-79

MEDITERRANEAN SEA

SEA OF
GALILEE

NAZARETH

JERUSALEM

BETHLEHEM

DEAD SEA

HILL COUNTRY
OF JUDEA

December 13th

A Prayer Against Hurry

Luke 1:39-40
*³⁹ At that time **Mary got ready and hurried** to a town in the hill country of Judea, ⁴⁰ where she entered Zechariah's home and greeted Elizabeth.*

TODAY'S PRAYER:

God, as my calendar gets closer to Christmas, the busier it becomes. In between Christmas parties and Christmas shopping, I'm fighting Christmas traffic in Christmas weather. If I'm honest, Lord, the stress of my schedule makes it hard to celebrate that silent night in the little town of Bethlehem.

I read in your Word that Mary rushed to her relative's home. But her hurry was not in a dozen different directions, her hurry was focused on being ready for you. She said *no* to so many of her plans because she said *yes* to you and being ready for your Son's arrival.

This Christmas season, help me to seek you first, before all things. To arrange my calendar to first prepare for you and let everything else be second. And then, Lord, would you show me what I need to let go of this year? What is frivolous? What detracts from a focus on your Son? After I create time and space for you God, what else needs to be removed?

In Jesus' name. Amen.

December 14th

A Prayer for the Holy Spirit

Luke 1:41-42
*⁴¹ When Elizabeth heard Mary's greeting, the baby leaped in her womb, and Elizabeth was **filled with the Holy Spirit.** ⁴² In a loud voice she exclaimed: "Blessed are you among women, and blessed is the child you will bear!*

TODAY'S PRAYER:

Heavenly Father, no one rejoices in the birth of your Son more than your Holy Spirit.

In the Christmas account the Holy Spirit overshadows Mary, he leaps with John, he shouts with Elizabeth, he prophecies with Zechariah, he sings impromptu songs with Simeon. If I want to know the joy of Christmas, then my prayer is clear:

Fill me with your Holy Spirit.

Your ever-present Spirit is with me and within me; but I want to be filled with all the fullness of you. Give a good measure, poured out and running over. Let your Spirit have his way with me—giving faith, convicting, counseling, comforting, guiding, and bearing his fruit in my life.

As I celebrate the birth of Jesus, let your Holy Spirit celebrate within me with whatever unrestrained celebration he so desires.

In Jesus' name. Amen.

December 15th

A Prayer for a Humble Heart

Luke 1:43-44 (CJB)
*⁴³ "**But who am I**, that the mother of my Lord should come to me? ⁴⁴ For as soon as the sound of your greeting reached my ears, the baby in my womb leaped for joy!*

TODAY'S PRAYER:

O King of Heaven, when Jesus draws near to Elizabeth, she instantly recognizes her unworthiness to be in his presence; enough to join the refrain throughout Scripture and ask, "Who am I?"

As I glimpse your majesty, Lord, may my heart be humbled. Show me how impossibly short I fall of your glory. Reveal your strength and holiness, that I might realize the depth of my weakness and sin. Show me, as your Word says, how even my righteous deeds are like filthy rags in your awesome presence.

Show me these things, God, that I might appreciate your Son all the more. How he came in all his perfection, to me in all my imperfection. To grace me, not only with his presence, and not only with your forgiveness, but also the full favor of your Son.

As I draw near to the day of Jesus' coming, give me a heart that feels unworthy and overjoyed enough to also ask, "Who am I that my Lord should come to me?"

In Jesus' name. Amen.

December 16th

A Prayer to Believe

Luke 1:45
⁴⁵ *Blessed is she **who has believed that the Lord would fulfill his promises** to her!"*

TODAY'S PRAYER:

Heavenly Father, throughout Scripture you made promises to send your Son—That he would be born in the line of Abraham and David, and from the tribe of Judah. That he would be born to a virgin, in the village of Bethlehem. That he would provide a sacrifice for my sins and establish an everlasting kingdom.

I praise you, Lord of heaven and earth, for fulfilling every Christmas prophecy you spoke.

Give me faith this season, God, to believe you are faithful to all of your promises to me. Your promise to be with me forever, to not condemn me, to give me eternal life. Your promise to love me, defend me, and guide me. Your promise to give me peace, joy, and power. Your promise to send me, equip me, help me. Your promise to hear me when I pray!

Blessed is the one who believes you will fulfill your promises to them!

In Jesus' name. Amen.

December 17th
Praying Mary's Song

Luke 1:46-55
[46] And Mary said:

TODAY'S PRAYER:

My soul glorifies you, Lord, [47] and my spirit rejoices in you, my God and Savior, [48] for you have been mindful of the humble state of your servant. I will be called blessed forever, [49] for you, Mighty One, have done great things for me—holy is your name.

[50] Your mercy extends to those who fear you, from generation to generation. [51] You perform mighty deeds with your arm; you scatter those who are proud in their inmost thoughts. [52] You bring down rulers from their thrones, but you lift up the humble.

[53] You, Lord, fill the hungry with good things but you send the rich away empty. [54] You have helped your servant Israel, remembering to be merciful [55] to Abraham and his descendants forever, just as you promised.

In Jesus' name. Amen.

A Prayer to Share the Joy

Luke 1:56-58
⁵⁶ Mary stayed with Elizabeth for about three months and then returned home.

*⁵⁷ When it was time for Elizabeth to have her baby, she gave birth to a son. ⁵⁸ Her neighbors and relatives heard that the Lord had shown her great mercy, and **they shared her joy.***

TODAY'S PRAYER:

Father in heaven, just as Elizabeth's relatives and neighbors shared in her joy, I want to share the joy of Christ's birth with others. The joy you give is too great to contain, O God! Make my joy contagious.

Who do I know that needs that joy? Who is bound by anger or depression that you want to free? Who is disenchanted with the empty pleasures of this world? Let the weary world rejoice!

How can I share my joy with them, Lord? Is it an invitation, a gift, a greeting? Speak, Lord, your servant is listening.

As I share my joy with them, give them joy in response. More than a momentary excitement, I pray they receive the joy of true faith—a faith that rejoices in Christ's birth because the eyes of their heart open to believe in the truth of their sin, of your holiness, and of your forgiveness through Christ.

In Jesus' name. Amen.

December 19th

A Prayer of Praise

Luke 1:59-66

[59] On the eighth day they came to circumcise the child, and they were going to name him after his father Zechariah, [60] but his mother spoke up and said, "No! He is to be called John."

[61] They said to her, "There is no one among your relatives who has that name."

*[62] Then they made signs to his father, to find out what he would like to name the child. [63] He asked for a writing tablet, and to everyone's astonishment he wrote, "His name is John." [64] Immediately **his mouth was opened and his tongue set free, and he began to speak, praising God.** [65] All the neighbors were filled with awe, and throughout the hill country of Judea people were talking about all these things. [66] Everyone who heard this wondered about it, asking, "What then is this child going to be?" For the Lord's hand was with him.*

TODAY'S PRAYER:

God in heaven, like Zechariah, open my mouth and set my tongue free to praise you, this day. I have been silent for far too long!

I celebrate with all joy this Christmas because you are not a vengeful or angry God. You are for me, you are not against me. Every title you hold, and everything you do, is for my good.

Everything you are is good—you are the Wonderful, Counselor, Mighty God, Everlasting Father, Prince of

Peace. You are the Word made flesh. You are the Highest, Most Holy, Light of Light, Eternal Desire of Nations. You are God with Us, the Son of Righteousness.

Everything you do is kind—you have not forgotten or abandoned us. You are faithful to your promises. You are kind and compassionate. You graciously bless us. You are merciful to forgive us. You have not treated us as our sins deserve. You are kind.

In Jesus' name. Amen.

December 20th

Praying Zechariah's Song

Luke 1:67-79
*⁶⁷ His father Zechariah was filled with the Holy Spirit
and prophesied:*

TODAY'S PRAYER:

⁶⁸ I praise you, Lord, the God of Israel, because you have come to your people and redeemed them. ⁶⁹ You have raised up a horn of salvation for us in the house of your servant David ⁷⁰ (as you said through your holy prophets of long ago), ⁷¹ salvation from our enemies and from the hand of all who hate us. ⁷² You have shown mercy to your people and remembered your holy covenant, ⁷³ the oath you swore to Abraham: ⁷⁴ to rescue us from the hand of our enemies, and to enable us to serve you without fear ⁷⁵ in holiness and righteousness before you all our days.

⁷⁶ Like your prophet John, O God Most High; who went before your Son to prepare the way for him, ⁷⁷ use me to give your people the knowledge of salvation through the forgiveness of their sins, ⁷⁸ because of your tender mercy, God. Like a rising sun sent from heaven, ⁷⁹ shine on those living in darkness and in the shadow of death and guide our feet into the path of peace.

In Jesus' name. Amen.

BETHLEHEM

Luke 2:1-19

MEDITERRANEAN SEA

SEA OF GALILEE

NAZARETH

JERUSALEM

BETHLEHEM

DEAD SEA

HILL COUNTRY OF JUDEA

December 21st

A Prayer for Generosity

Luke 2:1-7

¹ In those days Caesar Augustus issued a decree that a census should be taken of the entire Roman world. ² (This was the first census that took place while Quirinius was governor of Syria.) ³ And everyone went to their own town to register.

*⁴ So Joseph also went up from the town of Nazareth in Galilee to Judea, to Bethlehem the town of David, because he belonged to the house and line of David. ⁵ He went there to register with Mary, who was pledged to be married to him and was expecting a child. ⁶ While they were there, the time came for the baby to be born, ⁷ and she gave birth to her firstborn, a son. **She wrapped him in cloths** and placed him in a manger, because there was no guest room available for them.*

TODAY'S PRAYER:

O, gracious God, how Mary's heart must have ached, wanting to give your Son the highest honor and finest riches to welcome you, and yet she wrapped him in the only rags she could afford.

But you were pleased with her offering because you do not measure the gift, you measure the heart that gives it.

May you be pleased with the offering I bring, God. Even the best I can give you is an offering far too small, but I give as I am able. Take my talents and relationships. Take my finances and my time. Take my voice. Take my will. Take all my heart, soul, mind, and strength.

You first gave your Son to redeem the world. Mary was the first to give in response. May my offering be fitting for such a story.

In Jesus' name. Amen.

December 22nd
A Prayer for Attention

Luke 2:8-12
*[8] And there were shepherds living out in the fields nearby, keeping watch over their flocks at night. [9] An angel of the Lord appeared to them, and **the glory of the Lord shone around them**, and they were terrified. [10] But the angel said to them, "Do not be afraid. I bring you good news that will cause great joy for all the people. [11] Today in the town of David a Savior has been born to you; he is the Messiah, the Lord. [12] This will be a sign to you: You will find a baby wrapped in cloths and lying in a manger."*

TODAY'S PRAYER:

God, as Christmas Day draws closer, I confess it's easy to become distracted. I find myself thinking more about last-minute gift ideas and travel plans than I am about the miracle of your Son's birth.

Like you interrupted the shepherds during their work, God, will you please grab my heart's attention this day?

Interrupt me with your glory.

You who shine with a great light on a people walking in darkness, do it again! Break through my busyness with the good news that causes great joy—that a Savior, the Messiah, the Lord, has come. That all the things vying for my attention in these busy days would lose their importance when compared to the great gift of your Son.

In Jesus' name. Amen.

December 23rd
A Prayer for Peace

Luke 2:13-16
*[13] Suddenly there was a multitude of the heavenly host with the angel, praising God and saying: [14] Glory to God in the highest heaven, and **peace on earth** to the people he favors!*

[15] When the angels had left them and returned to heaven, the shepherds said to one another, "Let's go straight to Bethlehem and see what has happened, which the Lord has made known to us."

[16] They hurried off and found both Mary and Joseph, and the baby who was lying in the manger.

TODAY'S PRAYER:

O Peacemaker, when your Son was born the angels pronounced peace on earth because you were now reconciled to a sinful mankind through the atoning sacrifice of your Son.

O Lord, bring me a peace that flows from this heavenly truce I have with you.

Make peace and reconcile my broken relationships. Make peace and bring me wholeness of in my mind and body. Make peace and give me courage as I face hardship or an uncertain future.

As I pray for myself, I pray also for those I love, that the angels' news of peace on earth may be true among us once again. Bring shalom. Make peace.

In Jesus' name. Amen.

December 24th

A Prayer to Treasure

Luke 2:17-19
[17] When they had seen him, they spread the word
concerning what had been told them about this child,
[18] and all who heard it were amazed at what the
*shepherds said to them. [19] But **Mary treasured up all***
these things and pondered them in her heart.

TODAY'S PRAYER:

Heavenly Father, on this divine night you gave the matchless treasure of your only begotten Son, that whoever believes in him will not perish, but have everlasting life.

As I gather in worship with your people this day, give us hearts to treasure this blessed thought!

May every song we sing treasure his name. May every instrument we play treasure his name. May every prayer, every reading, every greeting treasure his name!

Fill us with awe, with reverence, with joy for this great treasure, God. From the young to the old, from our exultation to our stillness, from our coming to our going, let every soul feel his worth as we gather in worship on this holy night.

In Jesus' name. Amen.

A RETURN TO JERUSALEM

Luke 2:22-32

December 25th

Praying Simeon's Song

Luke 2:22-32

²² When the time came for the purification rites required by the Law of Moses, Joseph and Mary took him to Jerusalem to present him to the Lord ²³ (as it is written in the Law of the Lord, "Every firstborn male is to be consecrated to the Lord"), ²⁴ and to offer a sacrifice in keeping with what is said in the Law of the Lord: "a pair of doves or two young pigeons."

²⁵ Now there was a man in Jerusalem called Simeon, who was righteous and devout. He was waiting for the consolation of Israel, and the Holy Spirit was on him. ²⁶ It had been revealed to him by the Holy Spirit that he would not die before he had seen the Lord's Messiah. ²⁷ Moved by the Spirit, he went into the temple courts. When the parents brought in the child Jesus to do for him what the custom of the Law required, ²⁸ Simeon took him in his arms and praised God, saying:

TODAY'S PRAYER:

²⁹ Sovereign Lord, as you have promised, you may now dismiss your servant in peace. ³⁰ For my eyes have seen your salvation, ³¹ which you have prepared in the sight of all nations: ³² a light for revelation to the Gentiles, and the glory of your people Israel.

In Jesus' name. Amen.

Made in the USA
Coppell, TX
19 November 2022